SYNCRETIC PHONETYMOLOGY
OCCULT GRAMMAR & LANGUAGE

Books by Jahn Hooks

Rebirth of the Neteru: Breath Awareness and Integration for a Lightheart

Urban Aghori: Siddhis in the City

Tantrik Rainbow Body Breathing

Gnostic Rastafari

Albums by Illuminati Congo

Illuminati Congo (self Titled)

All Eye See

Green Is All I Need

Health Wealth Knowledge of Self

Siddha Gita

All is Tantra

Innergalactic

7R

Island of Patmos

Niggativity

Delphi

SYNCRHOGNOSTIC PHONETYMOLOGY
OCCULT GRAMMAR & LANGUAGE

JAHN HOOKS

2018

Copyright ©-2018-Jahn Hooks
First printing-May, 18
Isbn- 978-1-387-75816-6

Illuminati Congo Publishing

Chicago, Illinois

Illuminaticongo.com

Table of Contents

SyncrhoGnostic Phonetymology 7
Occult Words of Grammar 13
Esoteric Alphabet 40
Victim Vocabulary 57
Word Up 61
Sources/Resources 62

6

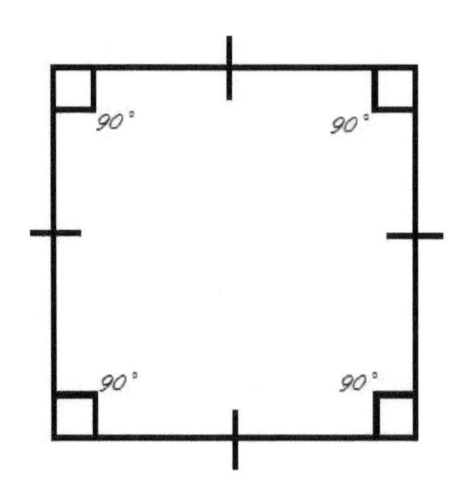

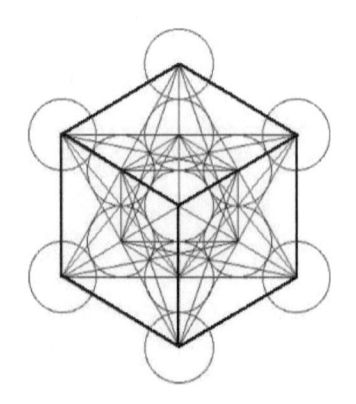

SynchroGnostic PHONETYMOLOGY

When different words sound similar or the same there is a connection through the sound resonance and the phonetics.

This is not folk etymology, nor an attempt to link similar words that have no historical relation.

Etymology is the study of the historical origin of words.

There is much value in standard academic etymology and this book is not an attempt to pass off connections between word sounds as historical links between different cultures or languages although some word sounds actually are connected historically.

The practice of appreciating word sound connections and invoking a workable meaning and application between such words is what I've coined **PHONETYMOLOGY**.

While etymology is the study of the origin of words, Phonetics is the sound the syllables make. So in the context of **Phonetymology** we consider similar and same sounding words and syllables, and how their similar sounds may provide insight or give us some substance to make such word sounds more meaningful for us when speaking, writing or thinking verbally.
If we don't imbue our words with meaning and value that resonates with us, they can't be used for our benefit.

Another new word/practice I am introducing here that functions dynamically with **PhonEtymology** is **SYNCHROGNOSIS**. Synchronicity is the providential alignment or a perceived harmonious connection of things and Gnostic is an inner intuitive understanding.

These two, **synchro** and **gnostic** combine to facilitate an intuitive wisdom, which is apt for using word sound power codes triumphantly. **SynchroGnosis** is not limited to our studies of **Phonetymology**. We can apply it anytime a meaningful connection brings itself to our awareness. Or whenever there seems to be a significant alignment of two or more normally separate seeming things or concepts. We view the appearing connections as infinite intelligence's entertaining way of inducing unity consciousness and inspiring us to experience our simultaneous oneness through multiplicity.

People who partake of cannabis tend to be more open to contemplate along these spirals of **synchrognosis**. Interestingly one of the words for cannabis can be found in the word syn**CHRONIC**. Utilizing **CHRONIC** makes connections in our brain synapses that seem to be reflective in our ability to find connections that weren't observed previously.

Applying a **SYNCHROGNOSTIC** approach when researching and working with **PHONETYMOLOGY** is essential for it to be of any value.

Etumo, the root in etymology means **truth** in Greek.
Log in etymology means **Word** as in **Logos**.
Etymology is the study of the word of truth.
But since words can't express truth but only point to it,

we utilize **phonetymology** to point to the truth but never mistake it for the truth.
The **word** or **logos** is **Vibration**.
The esoteric approach to etymology is **Phonetymology**, where we take the sound phonetics into significant consideration.

Phonetymology and **Sychrognosis** are complimentary systems of study and magick.

We use them to study and contemplate language, alphabets, speech, signs and **symbols**.

A **Symbol** is an image that represents something. A **cymbal** is a vibrating instrument that produces sound. The **Cym** in cymbal is the root of **CYM**atics that is research into how sound produces shapes and form. **CYM** means wave. All shapes are **symbols** with their origin in sound waves similar to **cymbal**.

Through our studies, the connections that pop out as relevant to us are asking for us to evoke a meaning that resonates between the word sounds, their common definition and our own will and imagination. The connection we just made previously between **Cymbal** and **Symbol** is an example of **phonetymology** thinking.
Although these two words may have no historical connection, the **cymatics** and **phonetics** resonate and a connection can be heard and perceived that may serve you.

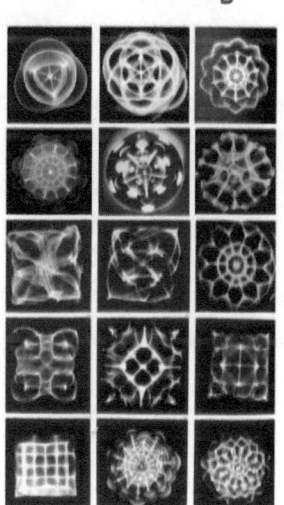

A personal meaning still connected to the popular meaning is generated that allows us to use the word sound or phrase more intentionally and meaningfully.

The specific words and combinations of words we use, the tone, the timbre, the intent, the attitude plus additional factors, all influence how our speech and writing shape our body, world, and relationships.

In this fairly short text we will explore the English language, alphabet and grammar all through the lens of **Phonetymology** and **Synchrognosis**.

Reevaluating English and grammar from this vantage point may reveal occult secrets of our English language. Yet it's also possible that all of the information and connections found here are irrelevant or don't connect for you.

The point is to find what meanings and connections resonate so strongly for you, that you are confident in your ability to use the magick word creatively and effectively towards your true will.

Here would be a good time to provide this disclaimer.

First a word of wisdom from Lao Tzu

"The Tao that can be told is not the eternal Tao; the name that can be named is not the eternal name. The nameless is the beginning of heaven and earth."

This scroll may be best appreciated as poetry and art.

All the words of this scroll are **illusory**. Everything I'm saying is **illusion**. Illusion has connections to **Illustrate, illumine** and **illustrious**.

Everything I'm saying is an **illustrious illustration** of the story within me. We all use **illusion** to **illustrate** our story. The whole universe is an **illusion/illustration** for the sake of telling the greatest story ever told.

Silence and emptiness are two words closer to truth. Truth can't be spoken or seen.

Truth can be said to be what is, without any interference of our senses and thoughts about what is.

So even these words I write aren't true.
The more words we write the further from truth we travel. This doesn't mean words are false or bad.

Words can be used to **illustrate** the most beautiful ideas of our imagination. But when we believe any **illusion** or **illustration** to be the thing itself we are in **delusion**. **Delusion** is **illusion** to ones detriment.

Illusion and **illustrations** by themselves aren't dangerous. Believing the **illusion** to have some source other than our own consciousness is **delusion**. In **delusion** people become manipulators and manipulated.

Words and language can be a major source of the manipulation.

Anyone attempting to control another through words is them self being controlled by their own delusional fear of harm or fear of not being good enough. Anyone controlled by another's words hasn't got deliberate about the magick inherent in their word sound power or has opted to be controlled.

When we return to Awareness that all **illustrations** or **illusions** are simply stories being produced from out of our consciousness we can better read and appreciate others stories as well as our own.

As we accept that we are the **Authors/Authorities** of our story, we are inspired to write stories with **illustrations** that serve others and us creatively and compassionately.
No more writing stories that aren't in our favor, nor reading stories that aren't our favorite type.

With that expressed, I urge you not to continue reading this text lest you are ready to receive this work from one **illusionist** to another. If you know you are an **illusionist** and that I am as well, this work will serve you. But if you are seeking to believe anything I am saying, you will fool yourself. Many who have begun a journey to explore etymology beyond academia and indulge in occult secrets have entered a wormhole of lunacy with no chance of return.

Proceed with this occult poetry responsibly.

Occult Language of Grammar

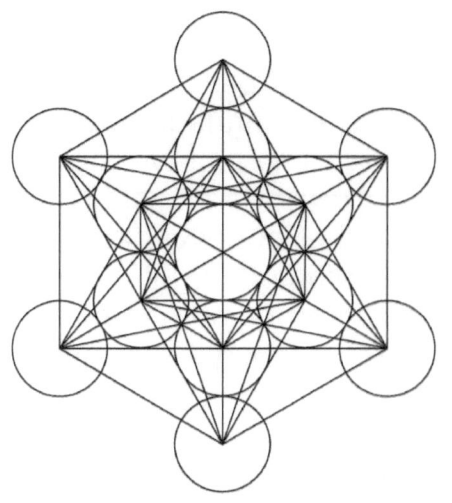

English has been called **Angleish** and **Angelish** referring to its occult phonetic connection to **angles, angels** and even the word **Ankh**(ang). We will explore the angle/angel aspect briefly later on. English is considered a global language. Its use can be heard and seen in most places on the planet, and the language most widely used on the Internet is English.

English is the language of international air traffic, maritime, policing and emergency services. Most scientific and technological information is express in English. 80% of all information stored in electronic retrieval systems is in English. English is the primary language of popular music and permeates pop culture.

Certain ideologies look at English as a bastard language. They claim it has no soul and that it is all borrowed from other languages. As far as having no soul, that is always dependent on the speaker. And the various languages that English is derived from are all powerful languages which when combined together could fuse a new alchemical product. Different ancient sacred languages merged to form one culminating elixir.

The God aka the aspect of our self, known as **Thoth**, **Tehut**i, **Hermes** is said to have created all letters, words, languages and symbols.

Thoth in this context can be considered the part of our brain, which uses language, speech, reading and writing. **Tehuti** is an aspect in all of ourselves that conjoined in communion, creating language to facilitate illusion so relationship can take place.

Since all is happening in Imagination, language is utilized to share our particular points of reference with some similitude of meaning to our imagined illusions. Thoth is also known as the magician in addition to being the lord of scribes and creator of words and languages. This is because language is a prime magick. Language is to **illustrate** through **allusion** and **illusion**.

The magician can **illustrate** whatever **illusion** is helpful to his true will with magick words. But the magician always knows the emptiness of the words. Magick wouldn't be possible if words were not empty and **illusory**. That is the source of their infinite potential energy. If not for the malleable nature of the empty substance we live in and as, we could not imagine, will and manifest. The empty **illusory** nature of all languages is one of their greatest virtues.

It would be impractical to attempt to share a breakdown of every single word in this work. Therefore what we are doing is laying a foundation that will allow one to appreciate the magick of the English language along with some basic framework for building ones own personal understanding and ability to utilize the ideas known as **phonetymology** and **sychrognosis**.

Old English was written in Runes. The word Rune means mystery or secret. Runes were used to **divine** and words made up of runes/letters are used to **define**. The connection between **Divine** and **Define** is significant.
Runes as an origin of our alphabet may reveal the original magical intent of our word and languages.

Some suggest Sanskrit as the first and original language, while others are sure it was Hebrew. Arguing which is the first or most special language is not productive nor is it a task of this text.

What I am intrigued by when studying any of the various ancient languages is that their original use in every case I've found has been for magick and their origin born from magick as well, according to the mythology. Also, the connection between similar sounding words, with related meanings in different languages, is thought provoking.

Sanskrit, Hebrew, Metu Neter, Runes, Phoenician Canaanite languages constitute the elements that form our present day English. These original spiritual languages are used to invoke and commune with or as divine archetypes aka **angels**. This relates to the meaning of the name of our language, English being an alternate spelling of **Angelish** as we proposed earlier.

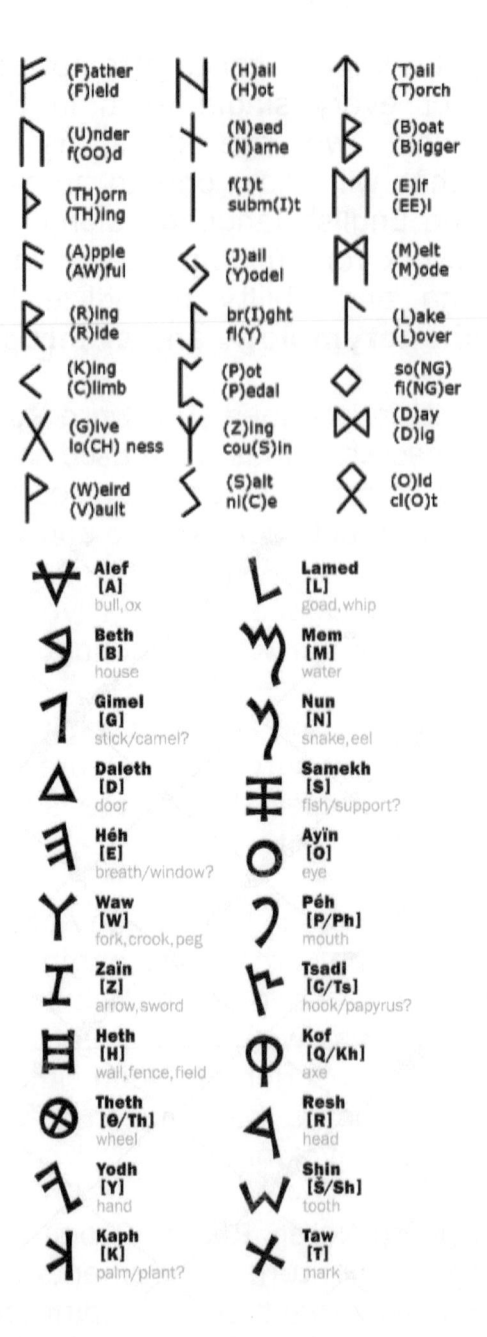

ᚠ (F)ather (F)ield	ᚼ (H)ail (H)ot	↑ (T)ail (T)orch	
ᚢ (U)nder f(OO)d	ᚾ (N)eed (N)ame	ᛒ (B)oat (B)igger	
ᚦ (TH)orn (TH)ing	ᛁ f(I)t subm(I)t	ᛖ (E)lf (EE)l	
ᚨ (A)pple (AW)ful	ᛃ (J)ail (Y)odel	ᛘ (M)elt (M)ode	
ᚱ (R)ing (R)ide	ᛇ br(I)ght fl(Y)	ᛚ (L)ake (L)over	
ᚲ (K)ing (C)limb	ᛈ (P)ot (P)edal	◇ so(NG) fi(NG)er	
ᚷ (G)ive lo(CH)ness	ᛉ (Z)ing cou(S)in	⋈ (D)ay (D)ig	
ᚹ (W)eird (V)ault	ᛊ (S)alt ni(C)e	⌘ (O)ld cl(O)t	

∀ Alef [A] bull, ox		L Lamed [L] goad, whip	
⊴ Beth [B] house		⋈ Mem [M] water	
⅂ Gimel [G] stick/camel?		⅄ Nun [N] snake, eel	
△ Daleth [D] door		⌶ Samekh [S] fish/support?	
⋻ Héh [E] breath/window?		O Ayïn [O] eye	
Y Waw [W] fork, crook, peg		⌐ Péh [P/Ph] mouth	
I Zaïn [Z] arrow, sword		⊬ Tsadi [C/Ts] hook/papyrus?	
⊟ Heth [H] wall, fence, field		⌽ Kof [Q/Kh] axe	
⊗ Theth [Θ/Th] wheel		⊲ Resh [R] head	
⅄ Yodh [Y] hand		W Shin [Š/Sh] tooth	
⅄ Kaph [K] palm/plant?		✕ Taw [T] mark	

If our language and lexicon is made up of various powerful ancient magical languages
Why wouldn't we consider it a prime tool for magick?

The word **Phonetic** in our system of **Phonetymology** is named after the **Phoenicians**, who's ancient language was syllabic. The sounds of the syllables are the letters.
Phoenicians are the offspring of **Kush/Ethiopia**. We can't neglect the Ethiopian connections to our English alphabet.

The word **spelling** and **spell** not only relates to **writing** letters out to form words. A **magic spell** and spelling with magic was the original purpose of words according to **Tehuti/Thoth**.

To **spell** is to cast magick energy with a definite purpose.
We **read papers** whose origin is **reed papyrus**.

Write and **writing** is significant as well. For it contains the word **Rite** as in ceremony or ritual. This word is usually related to secret traditions and initiations of passage, utilized to assist one in living magically. **Writ** means ones authority to command. What we **Write** is our **Writ**.

 Also the word **write** is the same sound as **right**. **Right angles** are **90°**. A square. This 90 or #9 is found in all sacred geometric **angles** in some form or another.

 The **word, word** itself has a few other phonetic relatives in this conversation. First, **World** and **Whirl**. The **word** makes the **world**. The **whirl** or spiral is the common natural geometry of the **world** as observed in the golden mean, Fibonacci sequence, the celestial movements, and the spiraling galactic patterns.

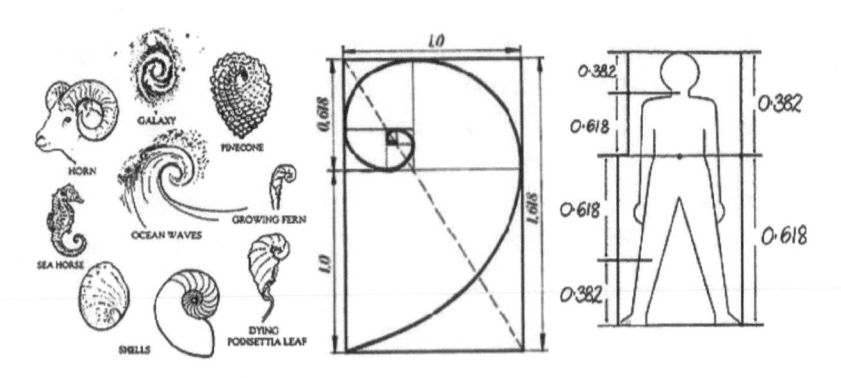

Word also is similar to the word, **wood**.
A **log** is a bulky mass of **wood**. And **Logos** means **Word** in Greek. In the bible book of John it says, "in the beginning was the **word**(logos), the word was with God...the word was God." The word **lodge** as in Masonic l**odge** comes from the word Logos. This is the only place the magic secret **Word** can be uttered. Considering Jesus who is called the **word** of God was said to be a carpenter who splits **wood** may be relevant to this view as well. The rings of a tree trunk look like ripples in water, and sound wave re**verb**erations emitting from a central point within a circle. **Woodwind** instruments and **wooden** drums are some of the first sound/music making tools of indigenous peoples.

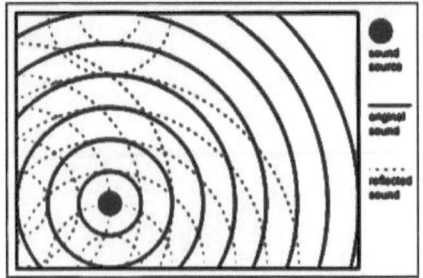

18

Wood relating to **word** surfaces again in **Timber/Timbre**. **Timber** is of course a form a **wood** and **timbre** is the distinctive character and influence of a sound vibration. The **timbre** is known as the tone color. Those with synesthesia May pick up on the **timbre** more easily. It helps us identify one sound from another.
Next we have the **Word, Verb**.
Verbum means **Word** in Latin so **verb** and **word** are one.

*Every **word**, and everything is a **Verb**.*

It is an eternal happening. Everything is in s constant state of moving, happening or being a **verb**.
Also in proto-Indo-European language **verb** meant Twig, branch or rod. All forms of **wood.** And **wooden** rods or **wands** are used often in the magick tradition. Re**verb** refers to sound **vibr**ations. Hear the word **VERB** therein.

Speak is traced to **specan/sprecan** from Proto-Germanic **Sprek** which can be linked with **sprig** which is a small stem bearing leaves or flowers taken from a bush or tree. This is another form of **wood**. The primary word for '**to speak**' in old English was **mapelian** or **maple**, another word linked to **wood**. The **word wood** backwards can be seen as **dow** pronounced the same as **Dao**. The **Dao** or the word that can be spoken isn't the eternal Dao or word. We can also hear the sound **do** in **wood** reversed as **doow**. This can be interpreted as saying what we **Do** with our **Words** or magick **wood** wand is most important not what we say. The **dew** nourishes the **wood**. To **do** nourishes our **word**.

Woden which is similar to **Wooden** is another form of the name **Odin**, a principal Norse God and Lord of Poets and is said to have created the Runic alphabet which English is intimately linked with. **Wedn**esday come from the word **Woden**, which is called meircoles in Spanish, because it is linked with mercury aka Hermes/Thoth/Tehuti.

Trees are made of **wood** and the **tree of life** is the kabalistic diagram/concept, which expresses all the letters of the alphabet in its branches.

 Would is the same sound as **Wood**. Would is related to the concept **WILL**. **Would** is the past tense of **WILL**. **Would** is also indicating the consequences of an **imagined** situation.
Wood is what we **would will** or have willed. Our **wants** are manifested with our **wand** and **wands** are **WOOD**. **Imagination** and **Will** are found in **Would/WOOD**.

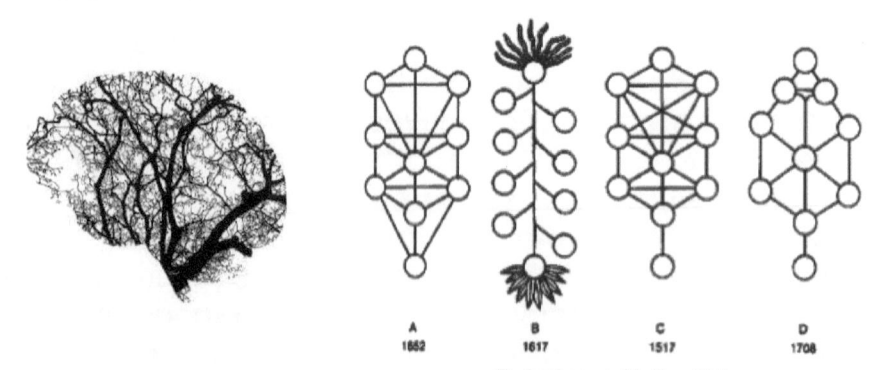

A
1652

B
1617

C
1517

D
1708

The Development of the Tree of Life

Sound comes from the Latin **sonus**. We see the word **Sun** and **Son** here. Son originally meant descendants not just a male child. This seems to suggest that we all descend from the **sun** and **sound** or a light color vibrational source. Even our **chromosomes** have the word **chrome** in it, which can mean Color or Tones as in the **chromatic** scale.

A **letter** is like a streamer or acceptance or one who **Lets**, or accepts, and allows. Letter says surrender and **Let Her**. **Letting** the infinite intelligence flow, **letters** form **words** or **worlds** with **whirling** chakra energy. **Let/Ter** is made up of **Let** (allow) and **Ter**(earth).

All that is **SEEN** or present on the **SCENE** is a **SIGN**. All **SIGNS** point to the un**SEEN**. All matter is vibrating and oscillating as a **SINE** wave and as **SOUND** else it would not be **Seen**. YHWH becomes the name of Jesus when it takes on **SIN/SHIN** ש as Jesus is said to have done. YH**S**WH. Ya**sh**uwah. To **Shine** with the **Sheen** of the **SUN**, may thine eye be **Sin**gle. The word **sign** is the root of **sign**atures and **SIGN**ALS, which are linked to magick word **signs** called **SIGILS**. Our **sign**ature is a **sigil**.

Letters are **Ladders**. We can ascend and descend the **ladder** of this illusory world utilizing the word with our true will as **Leader**.

Noun comes from **nomen** (name) in Latin. This can be traced to the Sanskrit **namah**, and **Namaste**. **Pronouns** connects with **Pranams**.

Namaste and **pranams** means to honor the divinity in a manifested person, place or thing. **Nouns** point to the divinity in all phe**nomen**a.

Phenomena can mean **Phi-Nomena** or spiraled into manifestation/**name**. It also contains the sound **Now**. **Now** is the only time we can be aware of the divinity in all **nouns** and **names**. **Nouns** encourage us to experience the divinity in the world of things **Now**.

Language and **Linguistic** is connected to Shiva **Lingam**. And the root contained in **language** is **ANG** (**ing,ankh**).

There are some interesting phallic links with **language**.
Dictionary and **diction** is connected to **Dick**.
Liber/libro is book and **libido** is sexual drive. **Liberty** or the freedom to manifest according to our unbounded will may be found in this book of words. **Leb** means heart in Ethiopian. Our heart is the **book** of the **law** (**Liber Lex**) and our **liberation**.

Semantics is connected to **semen**.
Semen is an anagram for **menses**.
A **period** is like the bindu red **dot**.
Another red substance that **dots** is called **period**. This **dot** also forms the point in the circle that represents RA. Interestingly the pronunciation is peer ee **YUD**. **Yud/yod** being the name of the smallest Hebrew letter, which is the first letter of the name Jah or Yahweh and Yahshuwah. In light of considering the **period,** which stops or stills a sentence, one is reminded of the biblical injunction Be Still and Know I Am Yah.

The word **grammar** can be found in tetra**Gramma**ton the magical Kabbalistic formulae.
The etymology of
GRAMMAR is seems to lend much credence to our point.

The old French form is
grammarye or **grammaire**.
The original definition of
grammar meant learning
incantations, spells, and magic.
In Middle English **grammar**
was known as occult
knowledge.

The Tetragrammaton

ヨYヨユ

Phoenician

ヨYヨz

Aramaic

יהוה

Modern Hebrew

The **trivium** and **quadrivium** are the 7 liberal arts and sciences of masonry.
(The **son** in mason and **sonic** in masonic could be hidden codes related to the masons use of sacred **sound**.)

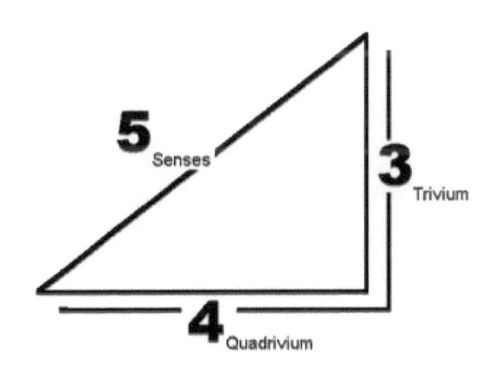

5 Senses
3 Trivium
4 Quadrivium

The trivium
Grammar
Rhetoric
Logic

The quadrivium
Music
Astronomy
Mathematics
Geometry

The **trivium** is obviously connected with language, while the **quadrivium** is less noticeably linked with it. Yet when one examines deeper the connections are there as well.

Music or harmonious **sound** is an element of **language**.
Studying the symbols and **language** that the celestial sky and bodies communicates to us through **Astronomy** lends to our understanding of **language**.

Mathematics is required for producing more than one **sound**. Therefore **math** is essential to **language**.
All symbols of language and shapes of letters have their root in a sacred **geometric** matrix, which we will demonstrate shortly. This makes **geometry** an active part of **language**.

Plus every **sound** we make with our **word** shapes the world around us. This is researched in the field called **cymatics** as mentioned early when talking about **symbols/cymbals**. Specific sounds create specific geometric shapes and influence matter in ways particular to their sound.

All letters can fit within a sacred geometric crystalline symmetric grid. It's as if all letters from all alphabets appear like the angles or symmetrical facets on a crystalline structure.

Lex means **law** with connections to **Lux** meaning **light**. An icon can mean an idol, a hero or **symbol** or a **sign**. Our **lexicon** aka our words and phrases can be seen as the **symbols** of the **law** or Maat and the **signs** of **light**.

Sentence comes from **sentience** and **sentire** meaning able to feel and **sense**. Feelings are essential for magick and **senses** are the root of all illusions. To speak or write a **sentence** has a magick purpose of communicating feelings that another can **sense** and feel. If two or more people can feel or **sense** the same or similar illusion, it becomes more real to them. A **sentence** is also a judgment or condemnation as it is attached to prison and death **sentences**. Judges decide the sentence and it's followed as **law**.
Every **sentence** we speak or **write** is upheld as **law**. It's a good thing our bodies are constantly speaking in our favor, lest our thought sentence would have condemned us.

We can hear the word **Spec** in **Speak**. **Specs** are lenses that we see through. The words we **Speak** internally and externally become this **Spec** or lens. **Spoke** is the past tense of **speak**. **Spokes** are the rods on the wheel of Law/Dharma connecting its inner axis to the outer edges. What we **spoke** goes around and around like **spokes** and becomes Law.

Syllable can be related to **Sybil** or **Cybil**, the mother of the gods in certain Greek legends. Her symbol being that of a pinecone. The syllabic sound tones that her name may be related to can activate the pinecone or pineal gland when used wisely.
Sound tone frequencies can be seen to be the mother or source of the god archetypes, as all forms have a **sound tone** at their base. A **mantra sound** is the base of a **yantra form**.

The sound **Owl** is in **vowel** and the **owl** is known to represent wisdom and the ability to see in, as well as embrace darkness. **Vowel** is made up of two words. **Vow** and **El**. **Vow** is to promise and **El** is a name for **God** or **light**. Each time we use **vowels**, we are repeating a **vow** to **enlightenment** and divinity. Words can't be spoken without **vowel** sounds. We are consecrating ourselves to and by source energy every time we speak. We are reaffirming our **vow** to **El** or **illumination**. **Vowels** sound like **bowels**. Our **bowels** are the core and organs surrounding our navel intelligence. **Vowels** are empowered by chanting from the **bowels**.

There are 7 basic vowel sounds in the Ethiopian and Greek languages. English only labels 6 of these sounds although all of the actual sounds are used in English despite not being accounted for in the naming of the vowels.

All the vowels combined together of any language to form one word, are said to produce a special name connected to divine source. By chanting this sacred name made up of all the vowels, greater illumination is experienced and able to be shared.

There are systems where The 7 vowels are linked with the 7-chakra energy centers of the body and through intoning the sound of each vowel, each chakra can be filled with bliss sound light energy. This helps maintain the whole energy body. In actuality there are more than 7 chakras as well as more than 7 vowel sound tones in most languages. The number of chakras and specific connections to different vowels may vary in some systems but that's fine. Explore which 7 sounds work for you. See if you like 8 or 9 tones too. Experiment with it. Some examples of 7 vowel sounds are...

Greek vowel sounds
A
Short e
Long e
I
Short o
U
Long O

Ethiopian vowel sounds
A as in mamma
E as in her
E as in chicken
EA as in get
I as in bit
O as in hot
U as in flute

Sound healing vowel sounds
Uh
Ooo
Oh
Ah
Eye
Aye
Eee

Vocal comes from the Latin **voc** and **vox** which have their origin in the Sanskrit **Vak**. The most simple explanation I can give for **vak** here is the ability to use **word sound speech** audible or not to create **worlds** and to be able to perceive the underlying truth and message any sound makes. As well as being able to sense the **sonic** vibration of any form.

The word **Para** means **supreme** in Sanskrit. **Graph** means to **write**, chart, or plot. A **Paragraph** is essentially smaller ideas that form one bigger **supreme** or main idea with an intention of charting a point of reference in the holo**Graphic** universe.

Compose is to **write** something in whole, and to be **composed** is to feel and express from ones whole being with a serene easy attitude, which is a major bonus to working magick. The **Compass** is used in masonry to circumscribe ones actions and in geometry to make a perfect circle. **Compass** is connected to **compose** and **compassion**. To **compose** is to **compass** or create from the point within the circle or as Ra. **Compassion** is requisite.

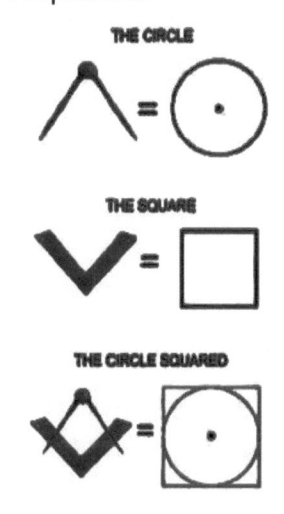

THE CIRCLE

△ = ◉

THE SQUARE

V = □

THE CIRCLE SQUARED

◇ = ⊡

Since **writing** contains **rite** and **right** within it, we can see the **right** angle square. And **compose** linked with **compass** reveals the **square** and **compass** as we **compose** any **writing**. This is why grammar is the first of the trivium and 7 liberal arts in masonic study. This square and compass is utilized for squaring the circle which we shall speak on further later in this text.

A **curse** is a magick utterance consigning an object to evil. **Cursive** writing contains the word **curse** and can be linked to creating **curses** or magick words to control or manipulate.

Pen and **pencil** come from **Pan** and **pentacle**. **Pan** and **Pen** can mean **one**, **all**, or **5**. And **pentacles** and **pentagrams** are magick tools used while **spelling**. **Pen** also meant feather. **Pluma** is a Spanish word for a **pen** and **feather** as feathers where used for **pens**. Maat, Tehuti's consort, has a **feather** as her symbol.

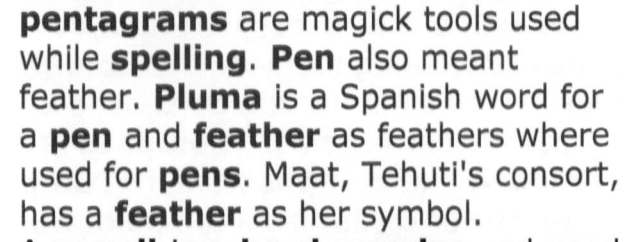

A **pencil** is a **hard wooden** rod used for writing and a **penis** is called a **hard wood** rod also. This returns us to **wood** and phallic symbology that seems to be built in to the language. **Pencil** is the **Pen Seal** or a tool used to draw or write a **pentagram seal**. **Drawing** is another form of writing. **Draught** is the same sound as **Draw** and it means to pull. When we are writing or **drawing** we are pulling and invoking from magickal substance.

The word **script** and **scribe** come from **scarab** dung beetle. The **scarab** or Khepera Khepri as it was called in Egypt Is used to represent Ra. It means Who Brings Into Being.

The scarab is also shaped like the human brain.

In human terms Ra is each persons power of presence to create in the now. We are always Ra and we are always creating.

Kriya means an outward physical manifestation of awakened kundalini. All that is **Kriyated/created** is a manifestation of kundalini. We are always experiencing manifestations of kundalini or the mother source energy aka always **Kriyating/creating**. **Create** ends with **8** or the infinity sign because **creation** is an eternal process happening in infinity.

The sound **KBLH** is found in **vocabulary**.
A **cabal** is a secret group. There is a secret **cabal** in our vo**CABUL**ary. **Boca** means **mouth** in Spanish. **Bocabulary/Vocabulary** comes from **Mouth**.

Kemetic texts express how the created universe came from the **Mouth/Boca** of **RA**.

The **mouth** is the symbol for the letter **R**, for the number 1 and unity consciousness in Hieroglyphics. The perpetual **kriyation** happening is maintained by **word sound** as the prime power and mover.

The old English for **mouth** is **moth**. **Moth** is an insect that transforms from one state (caterpillar) to another winged creature. Could the **mouth** and **word sound power** assist our ability to levitate and ascend?

The old German for **mouth** is **mund**. This is the root of the word **mundane** and **mandala**. **Mundane** is the world. A **mandala** is a sacred geometric image said to represent the **world**/cosmos. **Mandalas** are sacred symmetrical shapes similar to the images that appear when observing cymatics and the forms shaped by **sound**.

The **world**/cosmos is born through our **word**.

Our **word** isn't just **verbal**. The word **vibrare** is the Latin origin of the word **vibrate**. **V** is known as the number **5** in Latin Roman numerals. The **5** relates to human geometry and our connection to **PHIVE/phi/5**. The **ARE** at the end of **vibrare** is who we **Are**. Our **vibration** and alignment with **phi** (nature) is a primal preverbal **word**.

Word sounds similar to **we're** aka **We Are** aka **I AM**.
The **word** is The Great **I am that I am**.

 Tehuti applies **Hu Sia Heka** power of **Sound/Word**. Tehuti was said to utter Ra's words to create the world. Tehuti and his counterpart Maat in her form of Seshat the 'lady of the occult mysteries' are known as the Lords of the **Scribes** relating back to where we started this point, **scarab** being related to **scribe**.
Even the letters of Tehutis name in the Greek pronunciation seem to relate his secret code of **squaring the circle**.

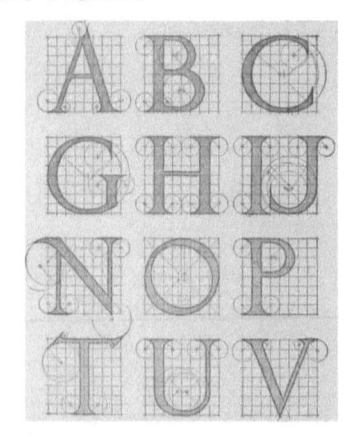

T H O T H an alternate form of Tehuti is made of Squares in the form of the **T square** and **H square**, 2 different tools of master masons. And the O or circle. Tehuti is known as Master of the city of Ogdad (8) in Khmunu (hermopolis).

All letter geometries can be seen superimposed on a squared circle. All shapes of letters may be viewed as different facets, faces or angles of a crystal. There has been some interesting experiments done by placing a small strip of a torus within a tetrahedron while shining light through the polyhedra, that have reportedly produced a reflected image of all the letters of Sanskrit, Hebrew, Greek, Tibetan, and Arabic. It is believed that all letters of every alphabet may be able to be generated this way. I recommend The Alphabet that changed the world by Stan Tenen if you'd like to explore this research in depth.

The vibrational **word sound** energies of Tehuti brought the creation concept (represented by the circle) into physical reality. This process is called **squaring the circle.**
The Egyptian mathematical principle of **squaring the circle** not only was used to develop all **alphabetical** systems, it is also said to have been used in conjunction with mantra incantations as an equation to build the pyramids.

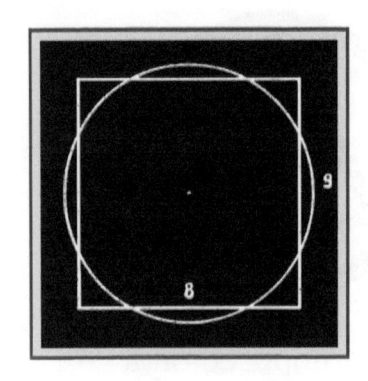

As was mentioned moments ago Tehuti is Master of the City of 8 and he is associated with the number 8. In the squaring the circle equation, 9 cubits always represented the diameter of the circle and 8 cubits the sides of the square.

9 represents the Neteru nine Gods who are one as Ra or the circular sun disc animating all creation with spirit solar force. And 8 represents the manifested world as we experience it. The 8:9 ratio is considered a perfect tone in KMT/Egypt and used extensively in many temples and pyramid architecture. The **letters** of our **alphabet** can be seen as born from the **squared circle**.

The word **THE** is short for **Theos**. **Theos** means **God** in Greek as can be seen in the words **theology** and **theosophical**. Also in Spanish **EL** and **La** mean **the**.

 El and **La** are both names of **God** and together make up the word **Allah** and **ELoh**
The word **Al/El** also means the sacred something, the affirmative, and **yes** in many languages of the east. While **La/Lo** means the sacred nothing.

Yes and **No** are reminiscent of the **yin yang**, which also are two aspects of The **ONE**.

I of course refers to the all seeing **eye** of the supreme self. Every **I** or being is the **eye** of God. **I** is also the same symbol as **1**. This speaks of our being **One** with source and All while simultaneously expanding Infinitely and Individually.

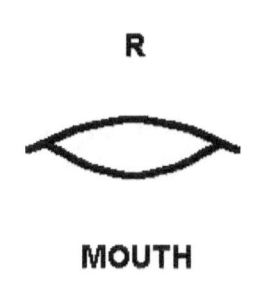

R

MOUTH

Our which is the same sound as **are** and the letter **R** is also referring to **our** unity consciousness and who we **are**, **individually** and **collectively**. The sound for **R** in hieroglyphics is written with a **mouth**, the same symbol for the number **1**. The letter **R** is shaped like the eye of **Heru**.

Here is related to Hera (Greek mother goddess) **Heru/Horus** and **hetHER** (Hathor/Het.Heru). To be here is to be composed of **matter** or **mother** or **HER**. The word **hours** can be seen as linked with the name **Horus** as well as **hero**. Anyone who is **Here**, in full present awareness is embodying **Heru/Het.Heru**, or being the **Hero** of their own story.

The Hero's Journey

Call to Adventure
Supernatural aid
Threshold Guardian(s)
Threshold (beginning of transformation)
Helper
Mentor
Challenges and Temptations
Helper
Abyss death & rebirth
REVELATION
Transformation
Atonement
Return (Gift of the Goddess)
KNOWN
UNKNOWN

35

The word **Is** is related to **Isis** as can be deciphered from this sentence itself. To say that something **is** or **is not** (isis knot) can never be known for sure. This is where the symbolism of the veiling of **Isis** comes from. **Isis** or what **Is, is** always veiled for the uninitiated.

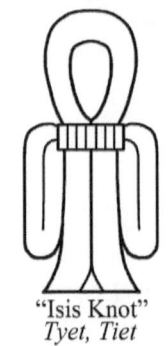

"Isis Knot"
Tyet, Tiet

May is a key to unveiling **Isis**. **May** is the root of the word **Mayat**, another **Isis** goddess form of KMT expressing as Truth Justice Order Wisdom. **May** means its possible. **May** does not act like it knows. **May** is possibility. **May** is synonymous with **Might**. **Might** not only means **maybe**, but it also means **strength**. Not knowing is wisdom and strength. **Isis** is unveiled when we come to the conclusion that what **Is, Is**.

When we say **its** cold outside, or **it** will be all right, or **It's** raining. Or **it** always happens, **it** feels good, or how is **It** going. What is the **it** we are talking about? **It** feels like the word **IT** speaks of the Dao or Life yet still represented in some tangible expression. **It** is the abstract being made objective. The word **It** is a great word for God as well, for **IT** does not lock one into outdated concepts, and it allows for change, expansion and variety. **It** is the eternity of perfection. **It** can be this, or **it** can be that.

That comes from **Tat** in Sanskrit which has been translated as '**all that is**" or Omnipotent/omnipresent/omniscient parabrahma. It can be found in the mantra
Om **Tat** Sat meaning "all that **is, is** truth"

The word **This** brings **that** closer. **That** is usually further. **This** is closer and personal. It is a combination of **The** or **Theos** and **Is** or **Isis**. Interestingly we also find the word **thesis** here that refers to a belief about some phenomena or principle. **This** and **That** are all beliefs we have of what **Is**.

The **OWL** is perched on Kn**OWL**edge.
Know reversed is **Wonk**. A studious person is called a **wonk**.
No is the same sound as **Know**.
Negation as in **knowing** what we are **Not**, leaves us with all there is left to **know**.
We spell **know** as in **knowing** with a **Now** in it because all that we can truly know is **Now**. The past can be remembered and interpreted and the future and be projected and contemplated but all we **know** is **now**.
Now in reverse is **Won** the past tense of **Win**. **Win** is the same sound as **when**, and **when** is always **now**.
Won is the same sound as **One**.

Notes are written words and it sounds similar to **know**. We use musical **notes** to express harmonious sounds. And the word **note** is an anagram for **tone**. Our **notes, tones, frequencies and word color our world**.

Metaphysics says thoughts are **things**. **Thing** and **think** are almost identical because any **thing** that's a **Thing** comes from what we **Think**. The **ing** at the end of **thing** express that it is not a static object but a **verb**, do**ing** or be**ing** or a happen**ing** intimately connected to what we **think** about it. Every th**ing** is constantly being recreated and is vibrat**ing**. And we Rite/Write our notes and words we th**ink** with **Ink** (**ankh**).

The word **of** has the root of the sound **love** in it. **Of** holds **nouns** within **nouns**. **Of** is the **love** that embraces whatever is spoken **of**.

The word **be** relates to **Being**. To **be** is to exist. **Be** houses whatever is spoken of in its existence. Everything comes out of **being**. If it is manifest, it must **Be**.

Also the insect, **bee** is called by the same sound possibly because it is a perfect example of how by just **being** itself, it helps spread **beauty** and sweetness thru flowers and honey all over. **Bees** are also sacred symbols in many magickal traditions. **Bees** are **buzzing** vibration that makes a sound similar to **B**. We also can **be** present to the humming vibrations and **buzz** our own magick **tones**. The masonic depictions of the beehive look strikingly similar to the pineal gland, and the bees buzzing surrounding can allude to sacred tones used to activate the pineal.

If comes from the Yoruba word **Ife/Ifa**. It refers to the **oracle** and divination sciences. **If** is always **rhetorical**. And **rhetorical** has the word **Oracle** in it.

And DNA. The word 'and' links information in a sentence or speech. The substance **dna** links information in our biology.

Heka is our ability to transform using proper word sound power.

Heka is the god of Magick in kmt.
Hex comes from his name.
A magick **hex** is another way to say spell.

Hex is the prefix of **hex**agon the six pointed star.

This is an upward facing and downward facing triangle United to form a **6** Point Star.

The **six** point star is a symbol for divine **sex** union.

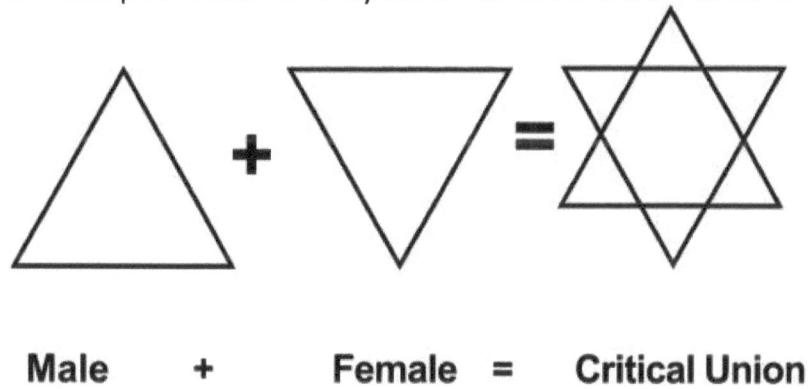

△ + ▽ = ✡

Male + **Female** = **Critical Union**

The word **sex** sounds like **six** and **hex** means **six**. **Sex** is one of the most powerful tools for magick.

Heka holds two snakes that form the letter **X** (found in se**x**/si**x**/he**x**).

X is the crossroads/portal where magick takes place

Esoteric Alphabet

There are **26** letters in the English alphabet.
26 is 2 x **13**. The Mayan calendar math is based on the numbers **13** and **260**. **26** is a sound number for working with sounds.
26 is the numerical value for **YHWH** in Cabala.

26 is the only integer that is one greater than a square ($5^2 + 1$) and one less than a cube ($3^3 - 1$). A rhomhioctahedron has **twenty-six** faces.

One possible way to build a bigger cube from smaller cubes is by laying 3 stacks of 9 cubes on top of each other, which equal 27.
This gives us **26** cubes that we can see, with 1 cube Hidden in the middle.

The one cube in the middle can be considered as silence since it is Hidden and can't be seen or heard.

The other **26** can be seen as representing the **26** letters of our alphabet. Silence is an occult hidden secret.

In the following **mandala** type diagram of the English alphabet we are expressing how the 7 heavens or celestial realms, the earth, and the 7 underworld levels can be seen as being born from **Word/Letters** coming from the **Mouth/Mound/Mandala**.

We can experience ourselves and our **world/mandala** as completely divine when we utilize our power of **word** to shape this malleable substance to our true will.

We display each letter within a tesseract like geometry to express a possible origin of these letters. There can be many sources that contributed to our present shape of letters. But as we said before, whatever connections resonate with us are for us, and whichever ones don't, are not.

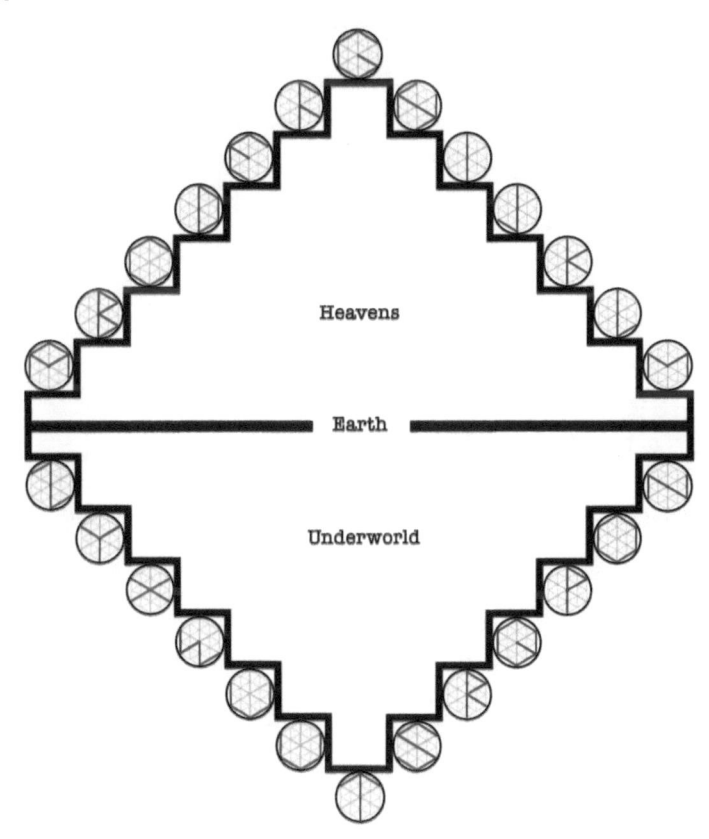

Heavens

Earth

Underworld

Contemplating this **diagram** (grammar of deity) could spark some **Phonetymology** and **Synchrognosis** connections for you.

This diagram of the alphabet appeared in my meditations one day while soaking in the bathtub. I knew it had special significance but the deeper explanation wasn't clear until I synchronized with Marty Leeds work while finishing this book.

He breaks down a Cipher in the English language connected to pi and squaring the circle that I feel I must include here. It was **synchrognosis** to see the pyramid diagram in my vision and then to find information from another source that seemed to explain the diagram in depth with mathematical precision.

Because it was **syncrognostic** how I cam across Marty Leeds pi, and the English alphabet, and because of how perfectly it corresponds to the vision of the image I had, I am including a portion here.

THE CIPHER
(From Marty Leeds Pi & The English Alphabet)

"Freemasonry is a craft and magick is real." – Claudia Pavonis

Splitting the **26** letters of the English Alphabet in half, establishing **13** letters per side (***A** through **M** for the left side* & ***N** through **Z** for the right side*) allows us to form symmetry and balance with our alphabet.

$$\text{SEVEN}_{65551=22} \quad 22 / \text{SEVEN} = 3.142 \, \pi$$

42

Using the motif of the **7** days of creation in Genesis (the six days of work with God resting on the seventh, or Sabbath – See Genesis 1 – 2:3, *Holy Bible – King James Edition*) we can assign numbers to the letters of the alphabet (**A1, B2, C3, D4, E5, F6, G7**) By resting on the **G** and the **7**th letter, we find a direct correlation to the Freemasonic symbol of the compass and square. The importance and meaning of this **G** within the square and compasses has long evaded scholars and masons. Its meaning becomes clear when we make this **G**, and its particular position in our alphabet, a central focus.

Walking back down to one from the **G7**, we can assign numbers to the remaining letters of the left side of our alphabet (**H6, I5, J4, K3, L2, M1**). To maintain our symmetry, or to create balance within our alphabet, we can apply his entire philosophy to the right side of our alphabet, **N – Z**.

ה + ו + ה + י = (26)
He Vov He Yod
5   6   5   10

THE TETRAGRAMMATON
The Holy Name of God using Hebrew *Gematria* Translates to Jehovah or YHWH

$\pi^7 \pi^7$ Pi begotten by 7 & Pi begotten by 7

Utilizing the symbol of the seven-branched Jewish Menorah, we can highlight our *non-prime* numbers (a prime number being a number divisible by 1 and itself) with those *non-primes* being **1, 4** and **6** and **6, 4, 1,** on both sides of our alphabet, with the central pillar resting on our **7** or Sabbath. Adding our nonprimes together, we find the number **22** (**1 + 4 + 6 + 6 + 4 + 1 = 22**). **22** divided by our central pillar of **7** equals **3.142**, a close approximation of pi found using whole numbers.

<pre>
        ABCDEFGHIJKLM NOPQRSTUVWXYZ
        1234567654321 1234567654321
</pre>

Combining both sides of our alphabet together, **22 / 7 = Pi** and **22 / 7 = Pi**, or ***Pi begotten by 7 and Pi begotten by 7***, forms what is known as the

Tetragrammaton, or the holy name of God, also known as *Yahweh*, **YHWH**, or *Jehovah*. *Tetra* means four, recognized in the four characters composing this great name in the Hebrew tongue (He Vov He Yod – shown on the next page), and *grammaton* is where we derive the English word *grammar*, confirming that this Holy Name of God is something that must be located somewhere within our language*, or our* **grammar**. *Not coincidentally*, in the Hebrew Gematria, the Tetragrammaton summed to **26**.

Using our cipher we can find the numerical equivalents for the two names of God found in the Holy Bible, **LORD** and **GOD**.
Notice both **Lord** and **God** sum to **13** recognized by the **13** letters on each half of our alphabet. Combining the two names into **Lord God**, we find the number **26**, recognized in the Hebraic Tetragrammaton as well as in the number of letters in the English Alphabet.

The English Alphabet was constructed using a *septenary*, or base-seven, system with **seven** being of added importance in its construction due to the central pillars of the menorahs resting on the seventh position, or the **G** and **T**. *Seven* has long been a number associated with esoteric, spiritual and mystical concepts. With the *seven days of creation*, the *seven chakras* and *the seven stars of the Pleiades*, the historical and mythological references to this most esteemed number are too numerous to count.

Using the English cipher on the number *seven*, we find the most astonishing occult gem. Hidden within the number seven, we find yet again, the transcendental ratio of pi. **SEVEN** sums to **22** and **22** divided by **SEVEN** equals **3.142**.

It would seem that the *transcendence* of this holy ratio of pi has been hiding beneath our language this entire time. And according to the symbolic representation of the Tetragrammaton, the ratio of pi seems to have a direct connection to this *Great Mystery* many of us simply call, **God**.

When we split our alphabet in two, we created a duality, or polarity, as well as symmetry with our **26** letters. This duality is found most prominently in the human realm as gender, or male and female. Much like the left and right hemispheres of our brains, we can assign the left side of our alphabet the masculine and the right side of our alphabet the feminine. By equating the halves of our alphabet to the male and female human being allows us to find, encoded within the numbers on each half of our alphabet, *a direct relationship to human anatomy*

LORD   **GOD**   **LORDGOD**
2 2 5 4 = **13**   7 2 4 = **13**   2 2 5 4 7 2 4 = **26**

```
ABCDEFGHIJKLM   NOPQRSTUVWXYZ
1 2 3 4 5 6 7 6 5 4 3 2 1   1 2 3 4 5 6 7 6 5 4 3 2 1
```

Marty Leeds Pi & The English Alphabet is a most excellent work of synchrognosis that will provide many intriguing connections that point to the divine magick of our 26-letter alphabet. Knowledge pertaining to the pattern of this diagram is explained in depth in his texts. I suggest reading them if you'd like to build upon this concept.

Here we are providing various meanings/interpretations of the letters in the English language. These meanings are sourced from many different origins such as KMT symbols, Vedas, the language crystal book, supreme alphabet of the nation of gods and earths, kabbalah and more. Many of these connections and meanings were born from my own **syncrhognostic** approach as well. Some links may not resonate for you and that is fine. Find what does resonate for you to bring more intention to your magick use of thought, words and writing.

A a

Specific individual creation
The one as two. Two united as one.
The first principle
Realization
Upward triangle
Allah
Two rays extending from one point.
The one point is being or spirit, and the two rays are body and mind united by the bar across.
Pyramid level building tool.
Strength,
Human being
Possibility
Beginning
Primal energy

" **ȧ**."[2] Seated God.

B b
To Be
Upward moving clockwise Spiral
Two separate
Born
The double neb of Nakhbet and Wadjet
13
Foot
Curvy and feminine.
Home
Nutrient
Intimate
Shelter

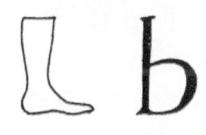

"**b**." Foot.

C c
See
Sea
C Mc squared
Light
Waxing crescent moon
Outgoing
Carry
Do good

D d
Do
Dios deity
Upward moving counterclockwise
Spiral
Delta curved triangle
Divine Destroy
First quarter moon
Combination of curvy and linear/feminine masculine
Door
Opening
Weaning
Descending flow

E e
Energy
Everything
Equality
Cubical grid
cubical matrix
Breath
Prayer
e spiral/sprout

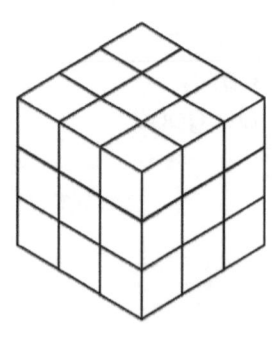

F f
Six
Father
Feather Maat
Fetha Law
Flag hieroglyphic neter/god
Phallus
Pipe

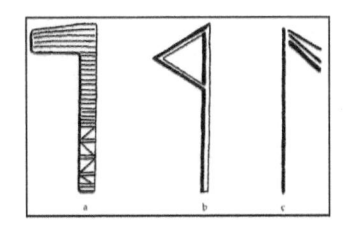

G g
Gravity
Geometry
Clockwise Spiral
God
Revolution
Change
Conflict
Contradiction

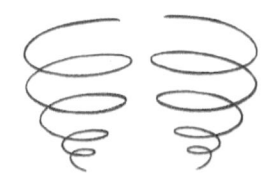

H h
Expulsion?
Ladder
He or her
Connecting parallels
Bilocation
Jump timelines
Enclosure

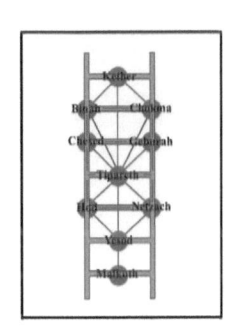

I i
Ego
Eye
I me
Islam
1 one
Uniting above and below
01 binary code
10
Hand
Give/take
Count
Time
Branch and sphere of tree of life

J j
Tree of life
Hook scooping the
sub-regions
Justice
Heka

K k
Life force
Synchronicity
King kingdom
Crown
Dua gesture
Blessing hand

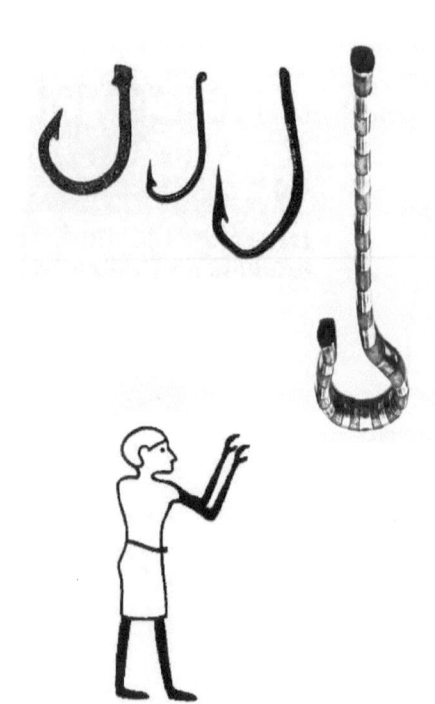

L l
90° square right
Love
1
Promote
Cause to move
EL/Light
Oppose
Study
Learn

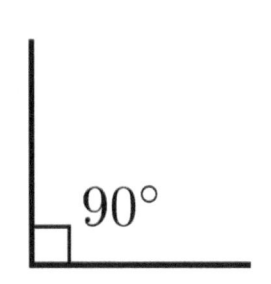

M m
Wave
Master
Owl
Water
Movement
Current

N n
Ending of wave
Now
Abyss
Hidden
Cobra
Snake
Occult
Fish
Infant
Stretch

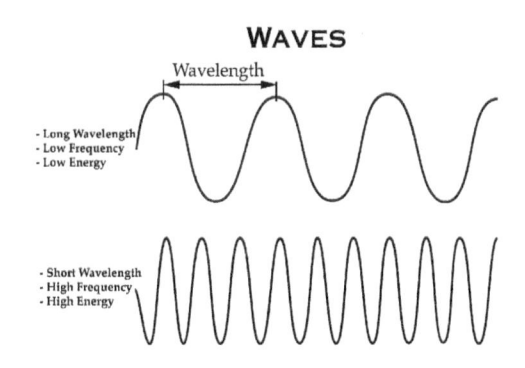

O o
Oxygen void femininity
Cipher
Full moon
New moon
Eye
Appear
Ring
Look
Gaze

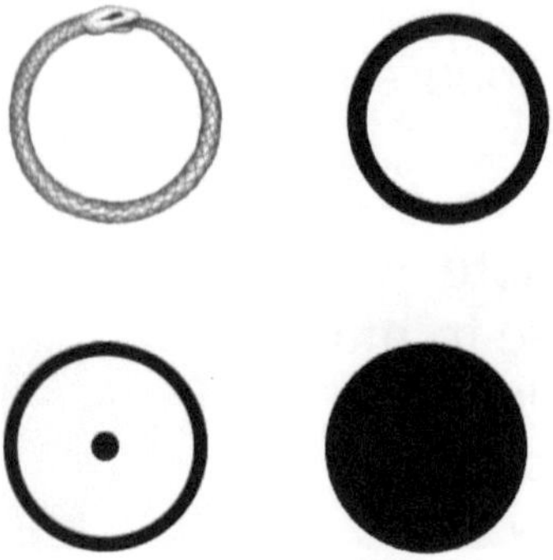

P p
Power
Downward counterclockwise spiral
Speak
Eat
Breathe
Exhale
Exit
Mouth
Female genatalia

Q q
Inside out
Torus
Downward clockwise spiral
Queen
Ape/Monkey
Eye of needle

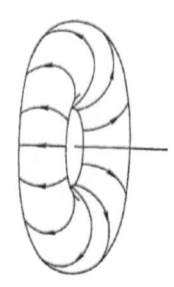

R r
Eye of R
Rule ruler
Uas scepter
Head
Brain create

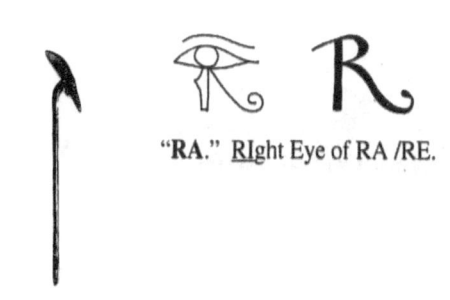

"RA."   RIght Eye of RA /RE.

S s
Serpent
Ascending
Self-savior
Attract
Emit
Transmit

T t
Crossroads
Truth
Square
Tau
Sign
Mark of alliance
Master Builders insignia
Breath and blood
Vital energy
Creative vacuum

U u
The crystal turning
Tuning fork
You
Universe
Horns Het.Heru

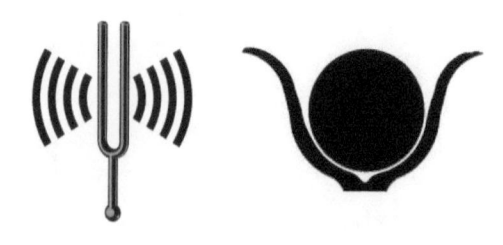

V v
Downward triangle
Vagina
Victory

Element symbols

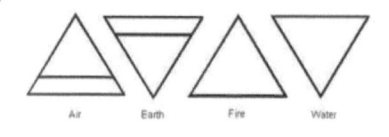

Air Earth Fire Water

Unity/Balance
All That Is

W w
Wisdom
Wave
Mandulis Nubian/kmt god crown
Trident trishul

X x

Unknown
Heka
Crossroads
Skeleton
Crossbones
Framework
Wood

Y y

Yoke
Yoga
Why
Tetrahedron

Z z

Zigzagzig
Buzzing
Lightening
Signature of Zeus and Thoth Hermes

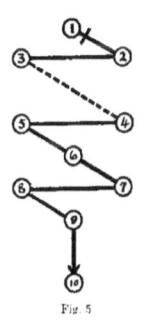

TAROT as CIPHER-TEXT

0	FOOL	△	א	OX / AIR		OX
1	MAGUS	☿	ב	HOUSE		TENT
2	HIGH PRIESTESS	☽	ג	CAMEL		FOOT
3	EMPRESS	♀	ד	DOOR		TENT DOOR
4	EMPEROR	♈	ה	WINDOW		"LOOK!"
5	HIEROPHANT	♉	ו	NAIL	Y	TENT PEG
6	LOVERS	♊	ז	SWORD		HARVEST TOOL
7	CHARIOT	♋	ח	FENCE		TENT WALL
8	JUSTICE	♎	ט	OX GOAD		SHEPHERD STAFF
9	HERMIT	♍	י	HAND		HAND
10	FORTUNE	♃	כ	PALM		PALM
11	STRENGTH	♌	ל	SERPENT		CONTAINER, CLAY
12	HANGED MAN	▽	מ	WATER		WATER
13	DEATH	♏	נ	FISH		SERPENT
14	TEMPERANCE	♐	ס	PROP		TENT PROP / THORN
15	DEVIL	♑	ע	EYE		EYE
16	TOWER	♂	פ	MOUTH		MOUTH
17	STAR	♒	צ	FISH HOOK		'CORRECT' PATH
18	MOON	♓	ק	BACK OF HEAD		ROTATION
19	SUN	☉	ר	HEAD		CHIEF
20	AEON	△	ש	TOOTH / FIRE		TOOTH
21	UNIVERSE	♄	ת	TAU CROSS	†	CROSS

Victim Vocabulary

There are words and phrases that seem to be disempowering, and rooted in blame, fear, guilt and victimhood. We will not be addressing all of them here for there are so many and that isn't the purpose of this book. There are other great books on this topic that are listed in my sources if you are interested further. It is my intention that by contemplating some of these disempowering phrases and words one will develop their own ability to assess whether or not certain statements and word selections truly serve ones purpose and vision.

Should and Shouldn't
Should and shouldn't are most often guilt programs. Thinking that I should do something implies I am wrong if I don't. Believing things should be a certain way or shouldn't be the way they are sets up self and/or others to be wrong. Could may be a better word that implies options. We could do things differently. If I want to offer a suggestion to another or self, it's much more resonant for me to say, "you could explore such and such" or "you may experience more pleasing results to explore a different approach".
You really should stop using the word should doesn't sound compelling.

I must/I have to
How could one be fulfilled doing something that they said they have to or must do? Who is making you? Anything you have opportunity to do is a potential for expansion and fun. Why not celebrate it instead of move along begrudgingly. You have to?
Id prefer I get to. I am thankful to do.

These phrases stimulate a begrudging lethargic attitude towards doing things.
Instead of celebrating what we can do, and what we get to do by saying "I get to go the post office." Or even more celebratory " I am thankful to wait in this line". I am blessed to be able to go to the post office, wait in line, and attend to my fulfilling business."

I can't
I can't has a victim vibration to it. "I am not going to" or I don't want to, or I wont are more empowering and truthful. Pretending like there is some force outside preventing you isn't helpful. Anything is possible for one willing.

Wrong
Seeing anything as wrong stems from duality and polarity consciousness. We can only label something or someone as wrong if we operate from fear. We label things wrong when we fear they can hurt another or us. The vibration of fear is the attracting factor for the hurt. We label people wrong if we can't accept their ideas or actions. Yet anything we are noticing in another is a mirror to us. Labeling another wrong only sets you up to feel wrong subconsciously. We can you like yourself when you are constantly judging your self in the form of other appearances of you called all of your relations?

Blame
Blaming is for people who stay focused on problems. Blaming is the age-old way to avoid taking responsibility to how we cocreate all experiences in our life. If you'd like to give your power away others, blame them. If you'd like to have a more fulfilling experience, take responsibility.

I'm sorry
I'm sorry is an affirmation declaring our sorriness and that we are a sorry person. Insulting ourselves to make another feel better isn't a wise use of words. We can apologize to others, and we can forgive and ask for forgiveness. But it's good to remember that eventually even forgiveness must be forgiven. To believe that another or we did anything wrong that requires forgiveness is guilt programming. When people communicate after perceived hurts it is helpful to acknowledge our responsibility in co-creating that experience. Forgiveness and apologies speak to this but if these are used in a context of guilt it will lead to more manipulation and degradation.

I can't stand this/I can't take this
This is a victim affirmation revealing resistance to what is and lack of acceptance. It also affirms an inability to stand in one of the statements, which could lead to leg, foot and standing problems.

I hate this
This is refusal to accept what is, and to be angry at it for being. Yet what we notice enough to hate is actually attractive to us. Hate is a form of fear is just like it's opposite called lust.

Week
Calling the 7-day segment week sets one up to experience weakness and lack of energy.

Morning
Calling the first part of the day upon arising morning sets one up for sadness and mourning.

Spend
Energy can't be created or destroyed. It's only circulated. We don't have to look at money as expending or as spending money. We can circulate money instead of spend.

Need
Anytime we say we need something we are making ourselves needy. Need entails lack. Declaring we need something reaffirms our need and lack. It may be more empowering to say, I desire, or I manifest, I create

Sick
Saying we are sick instead of affirming that we are healing shows where we place our focus. We can accept that we don't feel how most ideally would like to but calling ourselves sick isn't acceptance of what is, it is labeling what is as something that doesn't serve us. Calling any ailment or symptoms ours is also a lie. We do not own nor are in possession of any sickness or ailment. When one is getting well or healing a particular condition, we don't label it as sickness. And as soon as we feel other than our best, the bodymind immune and endocrine system works to bring us into greater harmony.

WORD UP

How we feel and how our presence stimulates others to feel is influenced by our self-talk and the word we communicate whether verbally, mentally or bodily. Everything is in the state of a **verb** or perpetual happening. What we intone and re**verb**erate through our field is what we experience. By applying our inking, speaking and thinking to thoughts that serve our True Will, our **vibr**ation resonates optimally for us. From this optimal point we work our word magick manifesting all we want with our wand every dusk and dawn. Synchronicity inspires Gnosis. Making connections previously unseen allows the brain to make new connections as well, within its tree of life branches synapses.

See what resonates with you.
Speak what resonates with you.
Imagine, Will, Attract and Create what resonates with you.

Sources and Resources for Phonetymology and SynchroGnosis

The Language Crystal by Lawrence William Lyons

Ethiopic, An African Writing System by Ayele Bekerie

Signs and Symbols of Primordial Man by Albert Churchward

Lectures on Ancient Philosophy by Manly P Hall

Heka, The Practices of Ancient Egyptian Ritual and Magic by David Rankine

The Angelish Dictionary by John Sacelli

The Cipher of Genesis by Carlos Suares

Egyptian Divinities by Moustafa Gadalla

Egyptian Harmony: The visual Music by Moustafa Gadalla

Mysteries of the Alphabet by Marc Alain Ouaknin

Blacked out Through Whitewash by Suzar

The Mystery of the Seven Vowels by joscelyn Godwin

A Mystical Key to the English Language by Robert M Hoffstein

The sacred word and it's creative overtones by Robert C Lewis

The Point Within a Circle by General Albert Pike

Sacred Sounds by Ted Andrews

The Esoteric Structure of the Alphabet by Alvin Boyd Kuhn

Rune Magic by Donald Tyson

The Concise Oxford Dictionary of English Etymology

English as a Global Language by David Crystal

The English Language by David Crystal

The Photoreading Whole Mind System by Paul R Scheele

Trivium and Quadrivium by Wooden Books

The Language Codes and Hidden Language Codes by R Neville Johnston

That Man up North by Phylotus

Pi & The English Alphabet 1-3 by Marty Leeds

The Alphabet that Changed the World by Stan Tenen

Unite ABOVE and BELOW as BELOVE

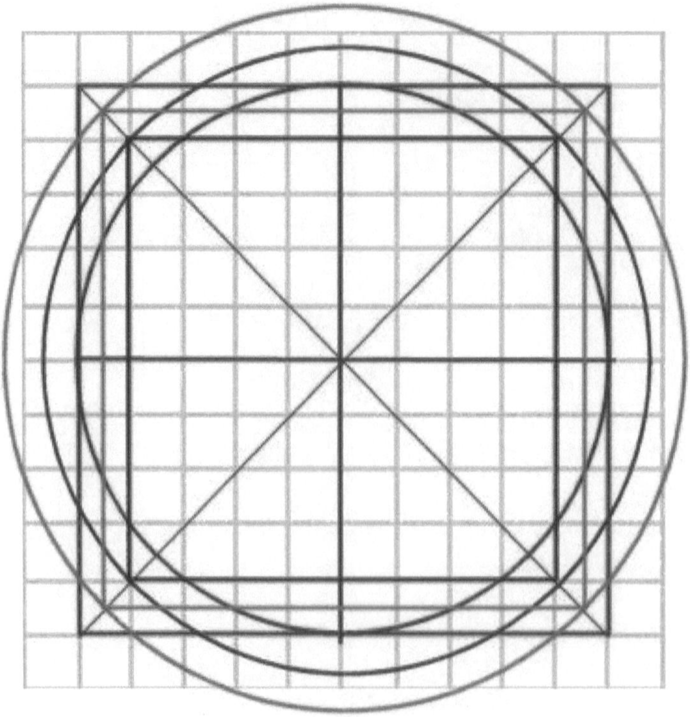

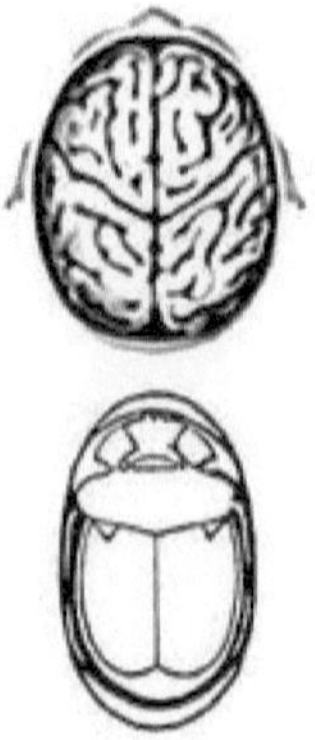